New Cambridge
MATHEMATICS

MODULE 3

Book 1

3.1 Doubling and lots more   *page 2*

3.2 Rain or shine?   *6*

A day of multiplication tables   *11*

3.3 Houses and homes   *12*

Faster and faster!   *17*

4.1 Fair shares   *18*

4.2 Shape changes   *22*

A day of 24   *26*

4.3 McMagic's sweet shop   *27*

3.1 Doubling and lots more

a Jumps

1 Kit jumps in 2s.

She lands on 2 4 ☐ ☐ ☐ . . .

Will she land on 20? Yes or No?

2 Now she jumps in 3s.

Will she land on 20? Yes or No?

She lands on 3 6 ☐ ☐ ☐ . . .

3 Try other jumps.

Do they land on 20?

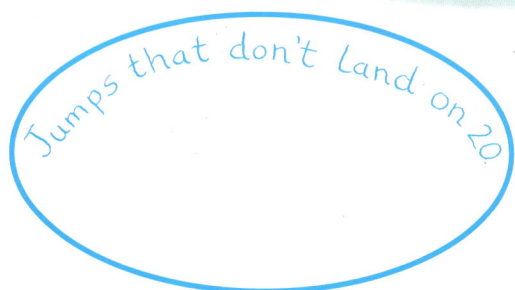

Try 4s

and 8s

Jumps that land on 20.

Jumps that don't land on 20

b More jumps

Investigate

Choose a number to land on.
Which jumps make Kit land
on your number?

51S

a Twos

1 Make sets of 2. Draw them.

b Two times table

1 Do **52**.

Practice

1 $3 \times 2 = \square$ $0 \times 2 = \square$ **3** $5 \times 2 = \square$ **4** $7 \times 2 = \square$

5 $\square = 4 \times 2$ **6** $\square = 6 \times 2$ **7** $\square = 8 \times 2$ **8** $\square = 9 \times 2$

9 Play a $\times 2$ game.

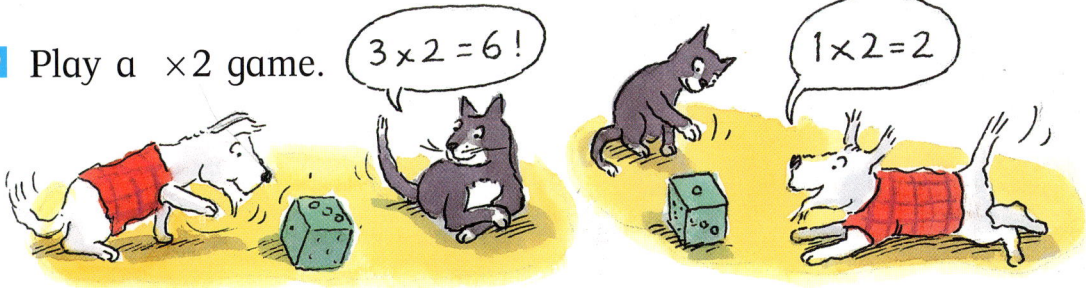

Mental maths

Say the $2\times$ table to a friend.

a Doubling

I know! Two fours make 8.

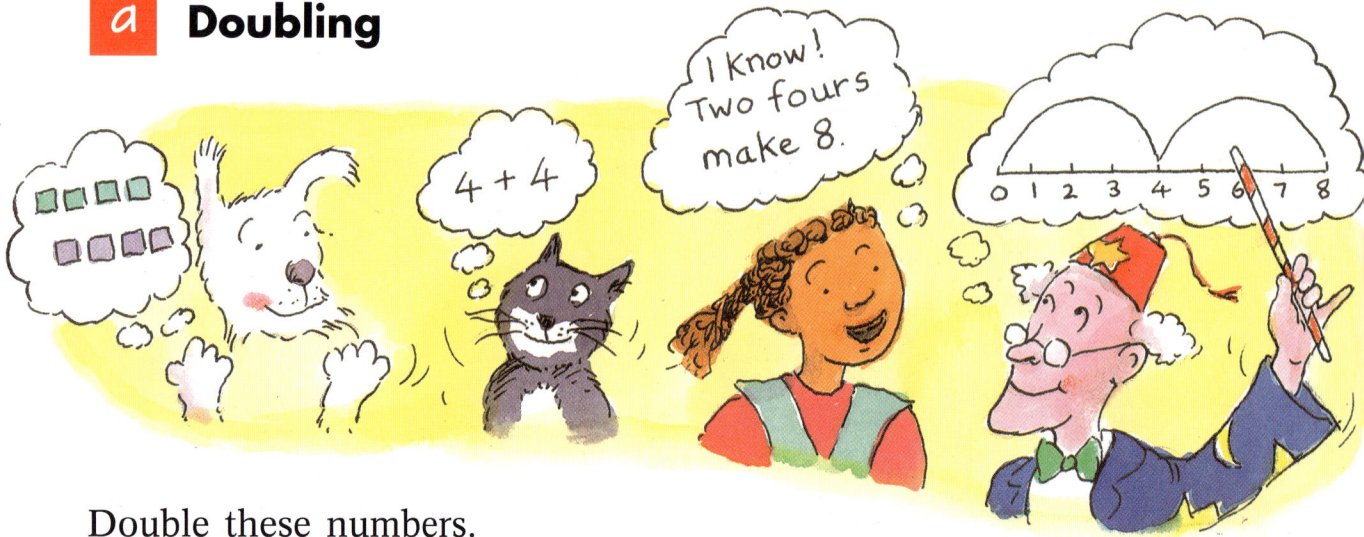

Double these numbers.

1 3   **2** 6   **3** 7   **4** 5   **5** 9

6 13   **7** 12   **8** 14   **9** 11   **10** 15

Make up your own!

11 ...   **12** ...   **13** ...

Can you do some really HARD ones?

b 4 socks for Nevis

I like 4 clean socks every day.

1 Nevis has 24 socks.

Does he have enough for a week?

Draw and write what you did.

2 Do 53 .

Practice
Write the 4× table.

53

a All change

It's 2 sets of 3!

You're both right. Look.

No it's not. It's 3 sets of 2!

$2 \times 3 = 6$ and $3 \times 2 = 6$

1 Do this with 8 cubes.

$\square \times \square = 8$ and $\square \times \square = 8$

2 Do this with other numbers.

10....15?

b The other way round

1 Do 54 .

Mental maths

1 2×3 **2** 3 lots of 4   **3** 4 lots of 2

4 5×2 **5** 2×5 **6** 3×2

7 Make up 5 more for your friend.

54   55

3.2 Rain or shine?

a   **Talk about time**

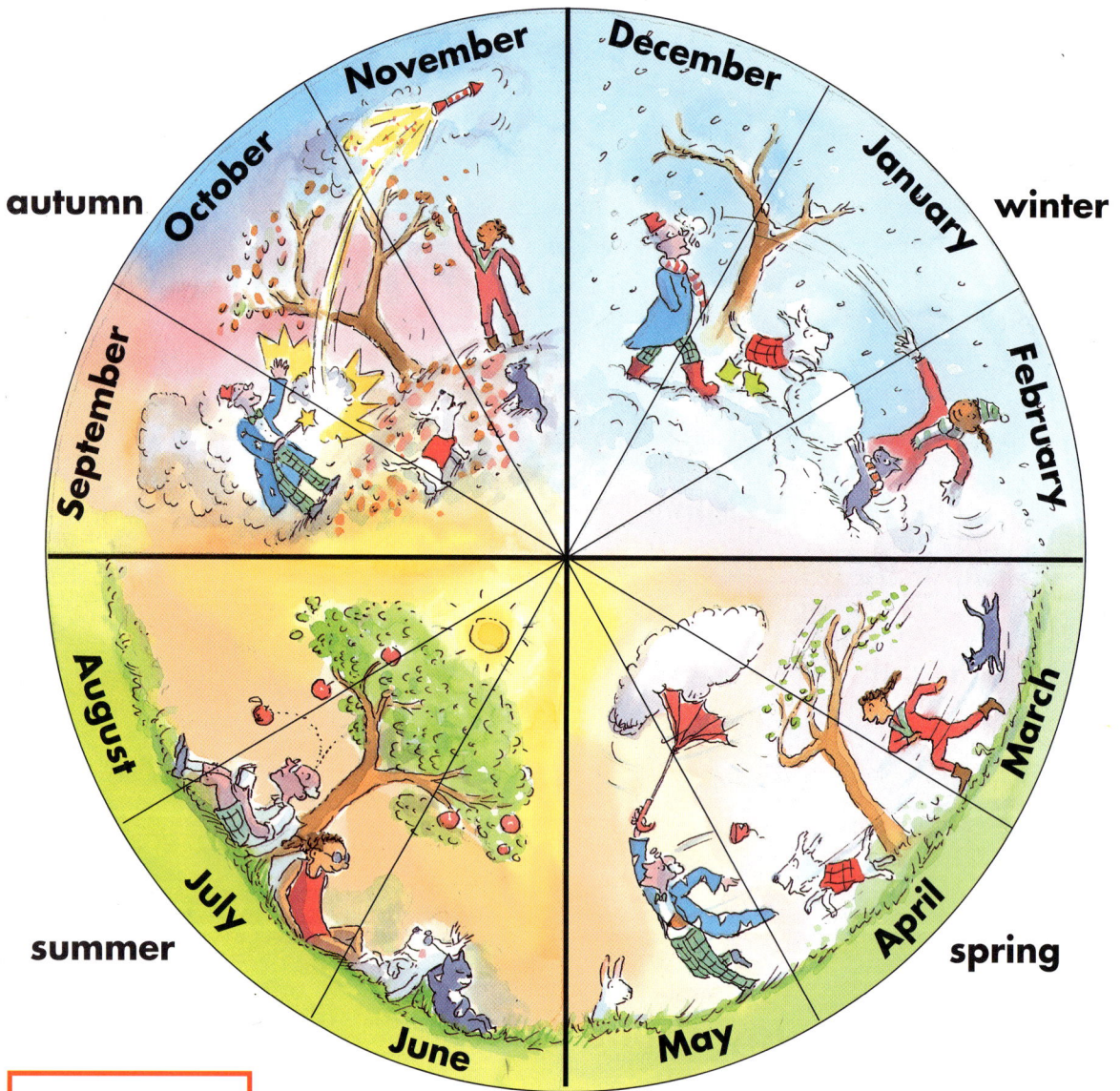

autumn

winter

summer

spring

November · October · September · August · July · June · May · April · March · February · January · December

Monday
Tuesday
Wednesday
Thursday
Friday
Saturday
Sunday

Thirty days have September,
April, June and November.
All the rest have 31,
except for February alone,
which has 28 days clear
or 29 in each leap year.

a Calendars

What are the missing numbers on this calendar?

APRIL				
Monday		7	14	21
Tuesday	1	8	15	
Wednesday	2	9	16	
Thursday	3	10	17	
Friday				

April
1 T
2 W Nevis's birthday
3 Th
4 F
5 S
6 Su
7 M
8 T
9 W
10 Th
11

Temperature at 9 o'clock.

April

Monday	Tuesday	Wednesday	Thursday
	1. ☀	2. ☁	3
	12°C	11°C	
7. 🌧	8. 🌧	9. 🌤	
10°C	11°C	12°C	

March/April
Monday 31
Tuesday 1
Wednesday 2
Thursday 3 Dentist
visit for Mr. McMagic

April
Friday 4
Saturday 5
Sunday 6

Notes:

1  What was the weather like on Nevis's birthday?

2 Do 57.

b A class day display

1 Make a day display and weather chart.
Change it every day.

a Talking about weather

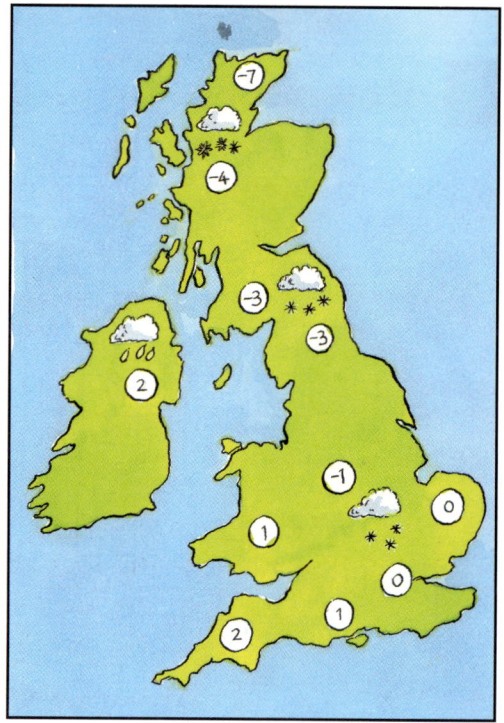

1 Which of these are likely the next day?

b What is the temperature?

Cut out the 5 weather pictures from **59**.

Put each picture with its thermometer on **60**.

Did you know?

Water freezes at 0°C.  Water boils at 100°C.

59 **60**

a Getting hotter, getting colder

1 Make your calculator count in 1s. 1, 2, 3, . . .

2 Start at 10.

Make the calculator count back in 1s.

I saw these numbers. □ □ □ □ □ □ . . .

Go past zero.

You might see this

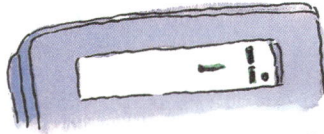

or this.

This is a negative number.

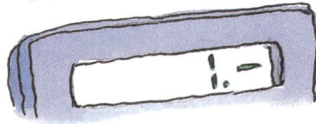

3 Write the missing numbers on 61 .

4 Start at 10.
Count back in another number.
Ring the numbers you get,
on one thermometer.

5 Count back again in other numbers.

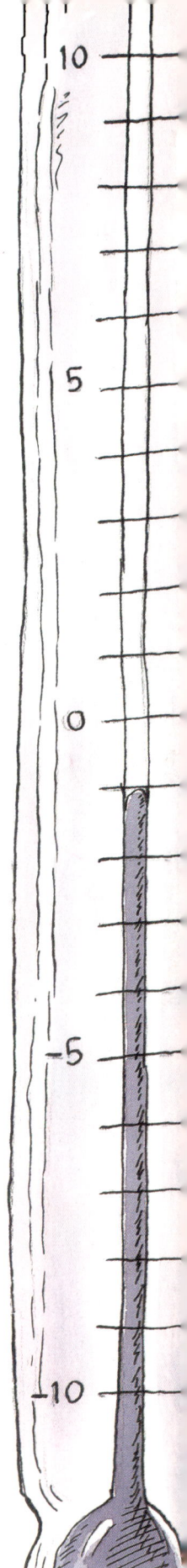

Try 2s.

I'll try 5s.

10

5

0

-5

-10

a   Recording rainfall

Rain has been collected in this jar.

The rain is halfway between 2 cm and 3 cm.

You can write 2·5 cm

or $2\frac{1}{2}$ cm.

1 Make some rain.

Stop when the level is halfway between 2 numbers.

We collected □ cm of rain.

2 Make more rain.

Stop halfway again.

We collected □ cm of rain.

b   Reading a scale

1 Do 62.

Mental maths

What is half of:

1, 2, 3, 4, 5, 6, 7, . . .

Half of 10 is 5 so half of 11 is...

A day of multiplication tables

a **Play these games**

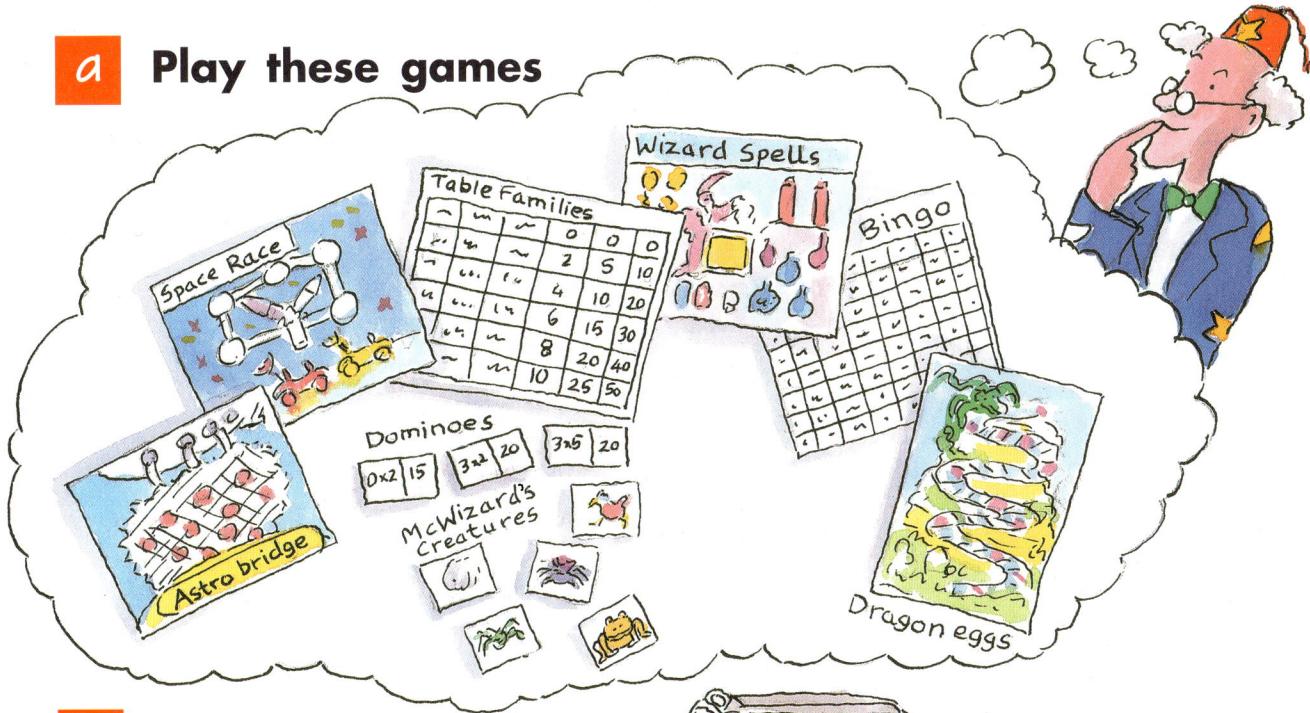

b **Journeys**

The buses take 10 people each.

The cars take 5 people each.

The bikes take two people each.

1 How can 27 people go
on a journey?

27 can go as ☐ lots of 10, ☐ lots of 5 and ☐ lots of 2.

You can't have empty spaces!

2 How can 12 people go?

3 Pick a number of people.
How can they go?
Give the number to a friend.

We worked it out in different ways. Did you?

3.3 Houses and homes

a The estate agent

1 Do [64] .

Draw a picture of the home.

b Homes database

> Home: Willow Drive
> Type: Semi-detached
> Number of bedrooms: 3

1 Make a record card about the home you drew.
Put it in the box with everybody else's cards.

2 Put your records on a computer database.

Your teacher will show you!

[64] [65]

b Playing estate agents

WIZZO Estate Agents

Can you find me a house with a garden?

and a cat flap?

1 Play 'estate agents' and find things out from your database.

We printed these from the database.

Houses | Prices

Gardens
Large
Medium
Small
None
1 2 3 4 5
No. of Houses

What do they tell us?

2 Do 66.

Building a house

1 Build a house with 3D shapes.

2 Sort the shapes like this.

good for building houses	less good for building houses

3 Now sort the shapes in another way.

Windows

This window is about 100 years old.

1 There are
- ☐ large panes
- ☐ medium panes
- ☐ small panes
- ☐ panes altogether

2 Do 67 .

67

Brick patterns

You need plastic bricks

1 Draw some brick patterns on squared paper.

2 Build these walls.

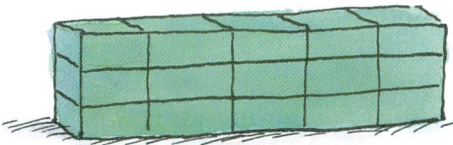

3 Which is stronger?
   Why?

How can you test?

4 Build walls with other patterns.
   Draw them.

a Journeys

The railway station has co-ordinates D8 and E8.

1 The school is in ___ .

2 The bank is in ___ .

Turn left by the library.

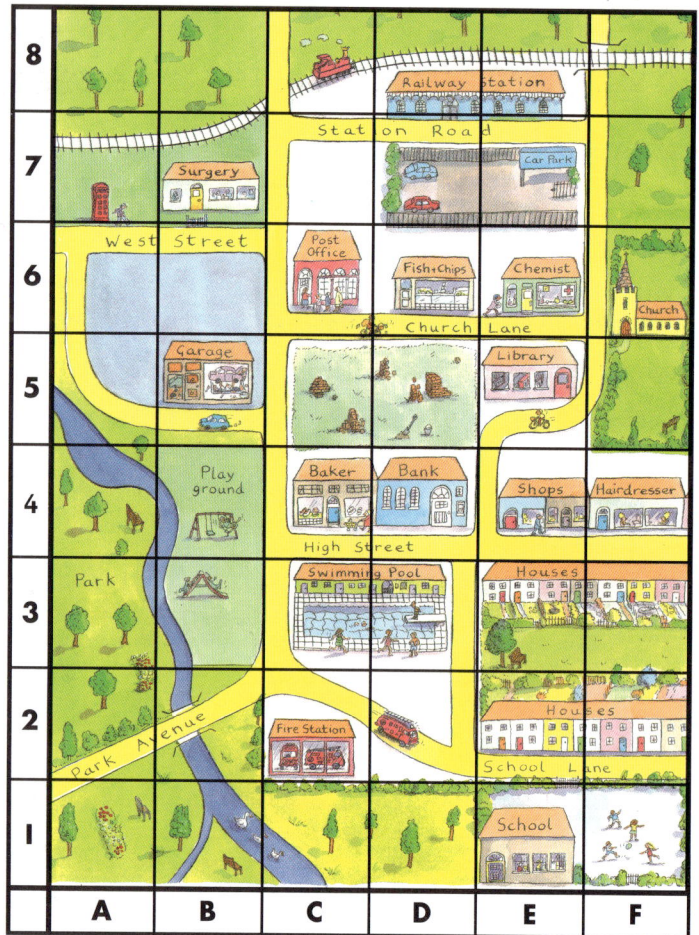

3 Choose somewhere to go.
Start at the school.
Tell your friend how to get there.
Write down the squares you visit.

C4

Is it in the park?

Is it in B2?

Is it in column D?

b Hide and seek game

Choose a square on the map
to hide treasure.
Write down the co-ordinates.
Keep them secret.
Your friend must guess.
They ask you questions.
You may only answer 'yes' or 'no'.

Faster and faster! (Mental maths)

A
1. $2 + 4$ 2. $6 + 1$ 3. $5 + 4$ 4. $8 + 1$

5. $3 + 2$ 6. $2 + 6$ 7. $3 + 3$ 8. $4 + 1$

B
1. $5 + 5$ 2. $9 + 2$ 3. $3 + 7$ 4. $8 + 2$

5. $7 + 2$ 6. $6 + 4$ 7. $8 + 4$ 8. $4 + 9$

C
1. $1 + 2 + 3$ 2. $3 + 4 + 1$ 3. $10 + 1 + 1$ 4. $6 + 1 + 2$

5. $5 + 1 + 4$ 6. $10 + 3$ 7. $10 + 6$ 8. $10 + 8$

D
1. $1 + \square = 3$ 2. $3 + \square = 5$ 3. $\square + 6 = 7$ 4. $\square + 1 = 5$

5. $10 + \square = 19$ 6. $4 + \square = 9$ 7. $6 + \square = 10$ 8. $\square + 6 = 10$

E
Use these numbers.   10, 5, 4, 3, 2, 1
Make up 8 sums like $10 + 5 = 15$.
Write the questions and the answers.

F
1. $10 - 3$ 2. $8 - 2$ 3. $7 - 4$ 4. $10 - 6$

5. $12 - 7$ 6. $14 - 7$ 7. $17 - 9$ 8. $13 - 8$

G
Use these numbers.   10, 15, 20, 25, 30
Make up 8 sums. Use + or –
Write the questions and the answers.

4.1 Fair shares

a Sharing

1 Draw and write this sharing story.

6 shared between 2 is 3. $6 \div 2 = \square$

Do the same for these.

2

8 sweets shared between 2 children

3

6 sweets   3 children

4

10 sweets   5 children

5 Make up more.

Practice

Do 68 .

b Use your calculator

1 $20 \div 4 = \square$ and $20 \div 5 = \square$

2 $18 \div 3 = \square$ and $18 \div 6 = \square$

3 $100 \div 2 = \square$ and $100 \div 50 = \square$

4 Make up some more pairs like these.

68

a McMagic's chocolate sticks

Nevis and Kit are making fun-size choc bars for the sweet jar.

They must be 2 pieces long to fit in.

1 8 pieces make ☐ bars of 2.

2 10 pieces make ☐ bars of 2.

3 12 pieces make ☐ bars of 2.

CHOP

| 1 | 2 | 3 | 4 | 5 | 6 | 7 | 8 | 9 | 10 | 11 | 12 | 13 | 14 |

4 Kit cuts this in 2s.

How many bars does Kit make?

b Counting back

Netty starts on 12. She flips back in 3s.

0 1 2 3 4 5 6 7 8 9 10 11 12

1 She lands on 9, ☐, ☐, ☐.

2 How many jumps did she make?

3 Do 69 .

Mental maths

Count back in 2s from 12.
Count back in 2s from 20.
Count back in 3s from 18.

a Nests and eggs

They divide the eggs into sets of 3.

1 Netty has 12 eggs. $12 = \square$ lots of 3.

She can fill $\square$ nests.

2 Kit has 15 eggs. $15 = \square$ lots of 3.

She can fill $\square$ nests.

3 Nevis has 9 eggs. $9 = \square$ lots of 3.

He can fill $\square$ nests.

4 There are 18 eggs left.
McMagic divided them into $\square$ sets of 3.

He can fill $\square$ nests. $18 = \square \times 3$

5 How many chocolate nests did they fill altogether?

a Backwards and forwards

Netty makes all these with 2, 5 and 10.

$10 \div 5 = 2$ $2 \times 5 = 10$ $5 \times 2 = 10$ $10 \div 2 = 5$

5 lots of 2 is 10
10 divided by 5 is 2
2 fives are 10
10 divided by 2 is 5

1 What can you make with 12, 4 and 3?

2 Find 3 more numbers.

b Do these on your calculator!

1 $\boxed{10} \div \boxed{5} = \times \boxed{5} = \square$

2 $\boxed{2} \times \boxed{8} = \div \boxed{8} = \square$

3 Make up your own.

Did you get back to your starting number?

It's like going forwards then backwards.

a McMagic goes round and round

Look at this!

You start here

6 × 2 ÷ 2 3

and go round!

Here is another!

8 × 4 ÷ 4 2

1 Do $\boxed{70}$.

Harder

2 $12 \div 3 = 4$. Write down what you would do to get back to 12.

3 Make up more of your own.

4.2 Shape changes

a **Look in the mirror**

These are symmetrical.
They balance.

These are not symmetrical.
They don't balance.

Kit made this model from cubes.

It's symmetrical.

Grr!

Nevis's model is not symmetrical.

1 Make a symmetrical model using cubes.

2 Make another model that is NOT symmetrical.

a Making symmetrical shapes

Make some of these.

1

Splot patterns

fold → drops of paint

Close it
Press it

line of symmetry

Open up to see your symmetrical pattern

2 Cut-out symmetrical shapes

fold   draw

cut

The fold is the line of symmetry.

Colour your cut-out shapes.

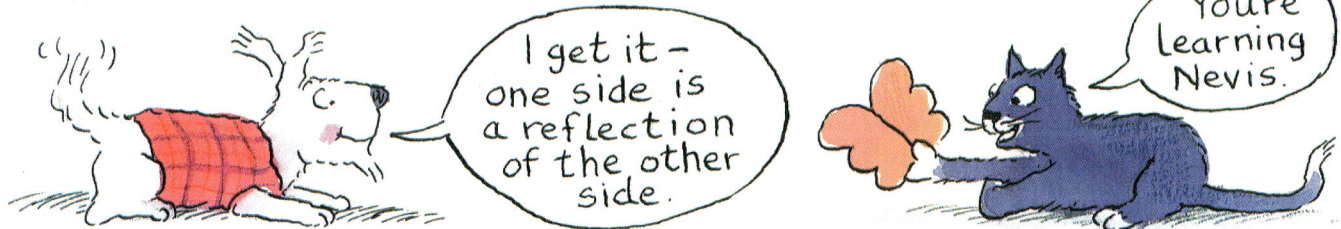

I get it – one side is a reflection of the other side.

You're learning Nevis.

b Polygon symmetry

Use a set of shapes like these.

Shapes

Find how many corners and sides each shape has.
Is it symmetrical or not?
You can record like this on 71 .

Which polygons have right angles?

Shape	Sides	Corners	Symmetrical
▲	3	3	Yes
▱	4	4	

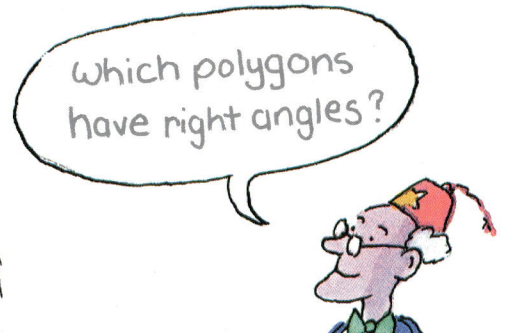

a McMagic's flipping fish

McMagic's fish can slide.

McMagic's fish can flip.

They flip over to make their own reflections.

1 Cut out a fish shape.

This is my favourite page!

Draw round it.
Flip it. Draw round it again.
Make this pattern.

. . . .

2 Which pairs of fish are reflections of each other?

3 Draw your own fish patterns.

73

a McMagic's changing shapes

Just three shapes, but what a lot we can do.

Kit's challenges.

Using just the two triangles   and
can you make:

1 a big triangle   **2** a shape with 4 sides   **3** a shape with 5 sides

4 How many different shapes can you make?

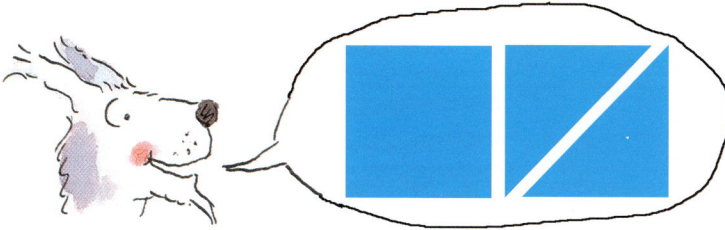

Use the 3 shapes to make these

5   **6**   **7**

8 a shape with 5 sides   **9** 6 sides   **10** 7 sides

Harder

11 Use the 3 shapes.

Make as many different shapes as possible.

Sort you shapes: symmetrical and not symmetrical

A day of 24

a Find 24s. Use 118.

24 sides

Can you find another set of shapes with 24 sides?

24

24th March

2p 2p 10p 10p

Can you find another way to make 24 pence?

$10 + 14 = 24$
$20 + \square = 24$
Find more

Arrange 24 in a different way.

Share 24 sweets fairly

b Get back to 24.

Start with 24. Secretly add on a number.

Can you get back to 24?

34

Netty must have added 10.

So I'll take away 10.

24

118

4.3 McMagic's sweet shop

a Counting money

McMagic likes to write money like this: £1·50

Time to count the money.

CLOSED

Nevis likes to count in pennies because it looks more: 150p

150p

It's just the same you silly dog!

1 Help them count. Do 75.

Kit makes up bags of 10p coins.
How many 10p coins are in each bag?

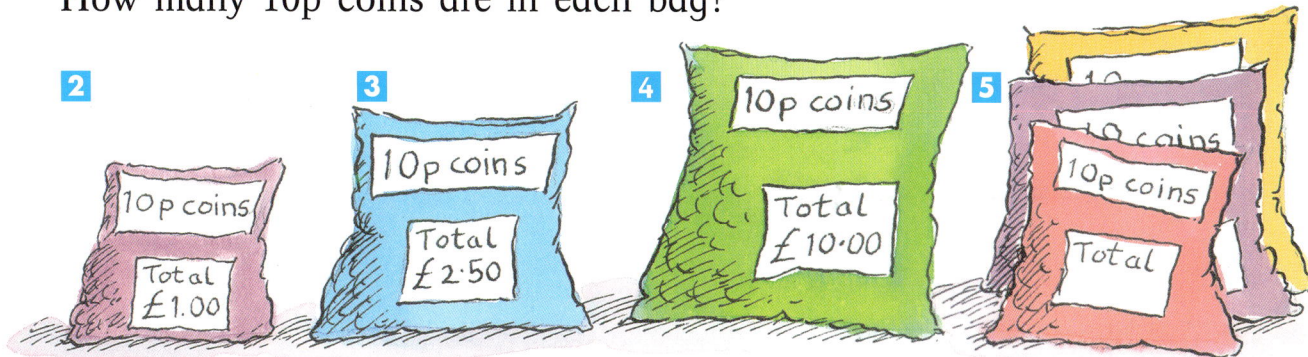

2 10p coins — Total £1.00

3 10p coins — Total £2·50

4 10p coins — Total £10·00

5 10p coins — Total

☐ 10p coins   ☐ 10p coins   ☐ 10p coins   Make up 3 more.

Investigate

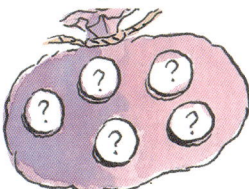

Kit had 5 coins in her purse.
She changed them for 8 (10p) coins.
What could the 5 coins have been?

Hmm...

b Bags of sweets

Netty wants to buy
some bags of sweets.

1 69p   She gives ☐ 10p coins.
She gets ☐p change.

2 85p   She gives ☐ 10p coins.
She gets ☐p change.

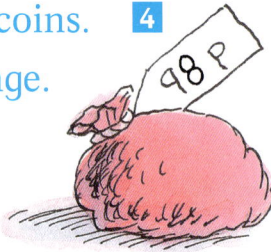

3 46p   She gives ☐ 10p coins.
She gets ☐p change.

4 98p   She gives ☐ 10p coins.
She gets ☐p change.

c Boxes of sweets

You have £1 coins and 10p coins.

How many must you give McMagic to pay for these boxes of
sweets?

How much change will you get?

1  £1·75

2  £3·47

3  £5·99

4  £7·68

5 Do four more.

a Inside McMagic's sweet shop

Talk about the sweet shop.

1 Do 76.

b Choosing sweets

You have 50p. Pick sweets from just two of the jars.
What mixtures can you buy.

1 Draw your own choices and write how much they cost.

2 Heather buys

30p + 20p + 6p = ☐p

She gets ☐p change from £1.

3 Ranjit buys

21p + 40p = ☐p

He gets ☐p change from £1.

4 Do 78.

a   What time is it?

1 The shop is open for ☐ hours in the morning.

2 It is open for ☐ hours in the afternoon.

3 The shop is _____ (open/closed)

4 Do 81 .

Shop open
8:30 to 12:30
1:30 to 5:30
Closed Sunday

b   Wake up Nevis!

I like a proper watch with hands!

He's so old-fashioned! I like my Wiz Dogs sports watch!

McMagic's watch says   Nevis's watch says

12:10   Wiz Dog

1 Use 82 to show these times.

	wakes up at	has breakfast
	1 quarter past 6	**2** 15 minutes later
	3 quarter to 7	**4** 30 minutes later
	5 7:00	**6** 15 minutes later
	7 quarter to 8	**8** 15 minutes later
	9 half past 7	**10** 15 minutes later

81   82

a McMagic's day off

McMagic wants to go on a
coach trip but he only has £5.

WizCoach Trips to:	Return fares
Trickytown	£3·00
Spell City	£3·60
Wandsville	£2·40
Beach Village	£5·50
Rocktown	£6·30
Fishy Point	£7

1 Where can McMagic afford to go?

How much change will he get if he goes to

      Trickytown   Spell City   **4** Wandsville

b Nevis tags along

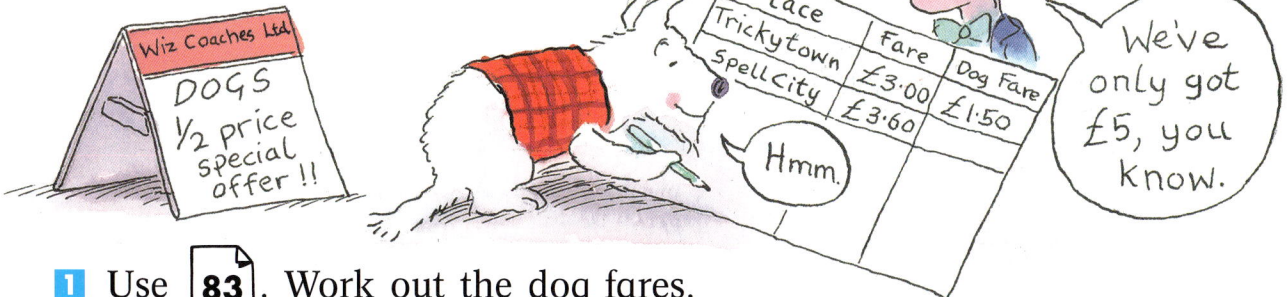

1 Use $\boxed{83}$. Work out the dog fares.

2 Where can McMagic and Nevis go for £5?

c McMagic casts a spell!

Now they have double the money. Use $\boxed{83}$ again.

1 Make a list of places they can go with £10.

2 How much change will they get?

a How long?

WizCoaches			Timetable	
Leaves			**arrives**	
Wiztown	8:00	Trickytown		9:10
Wiztown	8:10	Spell City		10:00
Wiztown	8:50	Wandsville		9:30
Wiztown	9:10	Beach Village		11:30

1 When does the coach to Wandsville leave?

2 When does the coach arrive in Spell City?

3 How long is the journey to Trickytown?

4 Nevis's watch says

How long has he got before the Trickytown coach goes?

b Catching the bus!

Nevis goes 'exploring'.
When McMagic finds him,
his watch says:

1 What time is it by McMagic's watch?

2 Which coach trips have they missed?

3 Which is the next coach to leave?

4 Nevis gets coach sick,
so he wants the shortest trip.
Which will he choose?